Do something different

Marcos Martínez

Marcos Martínez @euklidiadas

ISBN-13: 978-1514737583

ISBN-10: 1514737582

Marcos Martínez @euklidiadas

DEDICATION

I would like to thank everyone that, for the last year, has been there for me.

Marcos Martínez @euklidiadas

CONTENTS

Do something different

Do something different

Why have I written this book

Not long ago, one of my readers sent me an email after reading my blog (pensamientolateral.org) where he asked me to never stop being so "out of the box" . It seems that writing about such unlike topics from a different point of view helped him along his life.

This book covers steps that I have followed to reach my current state of mental awareness which has also been the spark to begin writing the blog, different profiles in social networks and the series that begins with this book.

I may warn you that during this writing period I have gone mad several times and while you read it you might have the same symptoms too.

This book can be classified as a self-help book. Nevertheless when you finish reading it, you might be the same moron that began it. Your improvement/development only depends on you. It is not a novel, nor it is one of those self-help books that will make you feel better once you finish it. This is a practical excercise book, you will only feel better if you follow my steps and try/discover something new. Or maybe not.

You have already tried learning a new language, going to the gym, changing your wardrobe, then why not following the steps of this book?

Bare in mind that you are making a mistake if you read this book in a single sitting. Reading it as if it was a novel will not help you. You will need to practice every day. Maybe that's a problema to you.

I don´t want you just to learn about yourself, I want you to have fun and be able to develop your own Lateral Thinking. And if you also become a better person, what else could you ask for?

You may have already read or checked other books that cover Lateral Thinking. Amazing books written by wise authors that also include great supporting drawings. The thing is, they all have just one single problem: Where are the exercises needed to progress? I have already read a few Lateral Thinking books and all of them are theoretical. Those books had a few classic exercises that didn´t work for me. And they didn´t work because they only offered one solution at the end, and that limits the possibilities. Therefore, it is not lateral thinking.

In general books about this topic are just a bunch of letters that explain the generic solution to each problem using sentences such as: "Only you define what you are" or "You are what you intend to be". If you want to be told those type of sentences, stop reading and keep on searching. Seriously.

As previously explained, sometimes you see online "Lateral thinking exercises". In fact, if you search on the Internet you will find hundreds. All of them have the same issues, they are guided activities with a single solution. Curious one, but single solution. The fact that is a curious but difficult to achieve solution doesn´t make the process of achieving it any different from the classical vertical thinking.

The entire book is a mind training guide. If I had to summarize this book in just two words they would be: **challenge yourself**.

If you are not up for running any risks, if you don´t want to see the world from a new perspective, if you dont want to learn how to learn, or to look for system mistakes, this is not the right book for you. What I am looking for is to introduce a new way for you to see the things that surround you using a set of challenges (or games) that I have personally used at certain points in my life.

This book is useless if you don´t put any effort. It is a book for you to learn. If you are not planning on doing the exercises please stop reading right now.

It is a highly participative book which only depends on you to learn.

What is Lateral Thinking?

Lateral thinking is the use of different channels to reach a diverging set of conclusions that may or may not solve the problem. Assuming that there a problem. It is not a way to solve problems, it is a way of thinking.

The term was conceived in 1967 by Edward de Bono, but this way of thinking has evolved for the past 50 years even though de Bono´s ideas are the only ones that seem to be online.

How is this book related to Lateral Thinking?

Along this book you will find some Lateral Thinking examples, although most of them appear only guidelines behavior, activities or challenges.

This is not a book of examples; it is a book that includes diverse activities that will change your day to day experiences and perceptions. I am assuming that to achieve different results you can not keep doing the same things. The only way to stop thinking vertically is to practice and train your brain to achieve it.

You will create your own examples as you go along the book.

Some chapters of this book are expression oriented (writting, meetings, speech giving, creating contents), others to companies (delegating, saying no to a job, even quitting the job), some of them to our family environment... At least, that is what it seems. All ideas within this book are applicable to all types of environments despite being classified.

What is NOT Lateral Thinking?

As previously mentioned there are dozens of websites and books that use directed rigid problems and unique schemes which offer no flexibility.

When I was small I used to like a problem that stated the following: In a complete closed room there was a dead man hanging from a rope. At his feet, three metres below, the room was full of water. There wasn´t anything else, no windows, no doors. How could the man be hanging 3 metres above the floor without any furniture?

The answer was that the water was earlier an ice block with stairs to climb. That was the answer with no other possibilities. That is not a Lateral Thinking problem. If it had been so, other posible no matter how absurd solutions would have appeared:

1. The ceiling wasn´t there before, neither the rope nor the corpse. A crane had put all of that at once in a roofless room full of water.
2. The man tied the rope using all of his strength because he had to climb the rope. He didn´t want to die of hunger or thirst. He died strangled because the the

badly design walls let humidity come through. With
humidity the rope shrank, increasing the distance of the
corpse from the floor.
3. There was loads of water before but it leaked around
the floor. The man decided to hung himself before
dying of starvation.

As you can see all of them are perfectly possible options,
maybe a little bit ridiculous, but also the problem is a bit weird,
isn't it? What I wanted to explain with this example is that
Lateral Thinking is a way of thinking not an answer restrainer.
For this reason is also known sometimes as Divergent
Thinking.

What am I asking you to do?

Don´t worry, it is not going to be any sort of offensive,
degrading or insulting stuff. I will ask you to work. As a
minimum you will need a blank sheet, and a pencil (or
whatever you prefer to write) in most of the exercises.

In other exercises you will need plenty of will power, and in
a very few of them even physical effort. Each of you will
improve as much as you can or want to. With 10 out of the 50
exercises I believe you can have a rough idea of what I am
suggesting you to do, but it´s much better to have different
options to choose from. And you totally deserve this, if you
have chosen to read this book it´s because there is something
you want to change. Thank you for choosing this book and not
other, thanks for this act of faith.

It is worth mentioning that without a personal analysis after
every chapter this book is pointless, you will laugh with some
of the chapters but you won´t get anything out of it. This is a
training book, and writing down what it has been achieved it
recommended.

What I do what I do?

Here is what you usually find in other books called as Introduction, but is it not boring that all books begin the same way? And more importantly, which example will I be setting if this book was the same as others?

First of all I would like to say that I learned the ocean´s movements through a novel, to see the world in a different way through movies and to behave through the people that surround me. It is important to observe everything to learn. But it comes a point in time that you have learnt everything from your environment and therefore you need a new one. This book will help you to do so.

When I was a kid I enjoyed writing, drawing, ("painting" when I can reach certain level of excellence), play with clay, and many more activities.. to all of them I always got the same response: "Stop doing foolish things and find a job". They meant it good, but that´s not what I wanted. I wanted to tell something to a lot of people. I would love to hear from someone: I learnt this from you.

I achieved this in a small scale when I was teaching as a private teacher for some High School and university students. What I taught them could be well obtained from school books and therefore quite boring and repetitive. So I said to myself: What hasn´t been written? What do I want my kids to know when they reach highschool or my dad before he goes to bed? What can I communicate that is not currently written anywhere else?

And if I have some expertise in something it is in seeing

Do something different

things from another perspective, give a new twist to things, asking myself if there is a better way of doing them. Or even a worse way, but other.

Basically, this book aims to go against the common practice, something I have always enjoyed. And I hope you do too.

Let´s get started!

Chapter 1. You read from right to left and from top to bottom.

I got that statement sticked to my head when I was small. The world is full of rules. It is so full that one of these days they will run over us and capture us.

I remember when I was learning the alphabet and I questioned myself the reason why it had been organized like that. What if that wasn´t the right order? It seemed that I was a little right because since I studied it the Spanish Royal Academy has destroyed two of the letters that existed: "ch" and "ll". I wonder whether the "w" will follow their steps.

Using the previous reasoning for this book means that you can begin reading it wherever you want. There is no before and after, there is no order. You can read it as it has been written or start from the last page. You can jump chapters. This is your book, so why don´t you read it the way you want to?

That's why you have entire Freedom with this book. I do not want to condition you in any way. , Moreover, if, when having finished this book (no matter if you have reached the end or just left it at the middle), you go against my thoughts, I will be pleased of discussing those with you. You will be able to do it in my blog pensamientolateral.org (in Spanish, I'm afraid).

But this is not only applicable to this book. A game I usually play is to read a chapter near the end of the novel before even beginning it. I know: you do not know the characters, or their role in the novel. But even before you don´t know them, right?

Doing this gives me a flashforward of information that, inevitably, the book increasingly tends to closer to the time. It is a way of alighting my curiosity from the beginning and ask what's going to happen next and what leads to that particular point and from there to an unknown end.

Why is this challenge worth doing? What do I get out of it?

You have been forced throughout your life to turn the pages from left to right. Today I encourage you to change your whole mindset and generate your own system. From the funniest challenge to the most boring one, reading random pages, following the established order: you choose. You have just earned autonomy and freedom, and you have not done anything but just reading a little.

And the best part is that you can apply it to almost everything: movies, books, magazine articles, talks. The flashforward beginning is not just for the film director or writer of the book. Now you can choose if you want to learn how to connect those points you've previously foreseen.

Chapter 2. The cistern that stopped working

I tried to flush the toilet at home and it did nothing. I swear that when I press one of the buttons the cistern emits a well known "blubb" sound and following that a stream of water that takes the shit out, probably to a river, then to the sea and, after evaporating, it will come back again as rain.

Because after pressing two or three times I did not get the expected result I decided to ignore the saying that goes "if you want different results don´t do the same thing." And I kept pressing the buttons fifty times in a crescendo of violence, until I convinced myself that there must be other ways to make it work rather than violence and intimidation by swearing. Something that did not seem to work too well either.

It was at that point when my head light went out. Probably several thousand neurons were suddenly disconnected, thus forging a bad idea. My followed this ¿reasoning?

1. Starting point: The cistern is not working
2. Diagnosis: It must be broken. If it was ok it would work, but it´s not.
3. Conclusion: I am sure it is broken
4. Measure to take: It needs to be fixed

If something needs to be fixed, every guy in the world knows what to do: take it apart, if possible with bare hands and with the help of a flat screwdriver or a non-sharp knife.

They say that engineering was born thousands of years ago to solve problems of society through technique, but I disagree with that definition. Clearly, engineering emerged from either two ways, probably both:

1. Engineering was born in an Egiptian bar, where a guy told another:

—It is completely imposible to pile up one of those bricks on top of another.

—What?!? —And then this lead ut to the Piramids.

2. Engineering was born as an excuse: When a child took his parents car apart scattering the pieces around the room using an allen wrench and his teeth, his alarmed parents went to tell him off, but then he said: "I'm an engineer,". "We have an engineer in the family", and they embraced each other without knowing what they had got.

Of course, they are not true examples, but I hope you like them more than the true and boring origin.

Returning to my original problem (the cistern), and still following the premise of "I'll fix this even if it´s the last bloody thing I do" I rolled up my sleeves and started to take the tank apart. To do so I opened the lid, I unscrewed the cylinder (now modern tanks come in compact cylinders to save water) and was about fifty minutes disassembling every pipe, thread and valve having no idea what was each and the function of the pump itself. I must admit that I still don´t understand it, and my pump is unlike anything that I have studied at college. To begin with, my pump has a lot more shit inside.

But to take the cistern apart was important!

It was a insult against me by the industry of homemade tanks, and I would not tolerate that my ability to play with those moving parts that multiplied on the floor of my bathroom was being questioned. Even though it meant a bleeding hand or having to buy a new tank because I broke it.

After playing with it for a while and not see that nothing was broken or messed up inside the pump decided it was okay, but it was possible that a piece had been released the last time it was flushed. So I proceeded to reassemble and put it in the tank, convinced that the mere fact disassemble and reassemble by expert hands would solve all my problems.

"If a computer can be fixed by turning it off and turning it back on, a tank can´t be that different"

That wasn´t the case. The tank was still broken.

In that particular moment, I went back to step 1: Press the 2 buttons for a long time, more than I will admit.

No change

Finally, I came to the following conclusion: I need technical assistance. So I went to the computer and looked for all the information I was able to find but I couldn´t understand almost anything and it was a waste of time. At this point I had been very good to have someone like Steve (Dave Barry's Complete Guide to Guys: A Fairly Short Book), but had none of them were nearby. "Steve" according to Dave Barry , are professionals who make home repairs and make you feel awful because they can do it and you can not.

Again, no change

So I jumped to the next step: I need help from a real person. So I waited for my father. He is a guy too, he even has several toolboxes that include hundreds funny gadgets such as screwdrivers, coils, small electric motors, a host of 50 different metric nuts, screws, nails, drill bits and other sharp objects to prove that.

But it wasn´t necessary for my father to come home to be drilled out to a table and, after all, to follow each and every one of my previous steps,. Because the water came back within a few hours. Turns out the tank was fine, but a pipe street had broken that morning, and as I dismounted my tank, qualified people (with great machines capable of opening holes in the street) solved the real problem.

Try to look beyond the problem today. Searching for the origin of what has happened to you. Most common problems are often a result of many factors. Try to see the full set and do not stay on the surface of the problem. A car is not broken because it is broken, but because it has not been properly maintained, or has suffered a lot, or because you have not used it as you should have...

Why is this challenge worth doing? What do I get out of it?

Does this example relate to you? How many times have you hit the computer mouse to go faster or yelled in your car to try to end a traffic jam?

Perspective helps us to see the real problema focus. And, in many cases, staring at it is the best we can do. Analyze each problem or situation going several steps back to the source of the problem. If you stay in front of a computer monitor that does not turn on is very unlikely that you will find out that the plug where it is plugged in is not working.

Chapter 3: How to make a fool of yourself. Do something scary, do it soon.

When I go out with my friends they usually say things like:

—Come on dude, speak more quietly.

—Stop doing that! —Quite hysteric.

—He starts again…

For some unknown reason, people keep using a concept that was not activated on me when I was born: shame.

Embarrassment is what will stand in your way and get you not to do something you want simply because someone else may think wrong of you. I'll tell you a secret: you cannot prevent people think of you what you do not want them to, even if you act one way or another. It is impossible. There will always be someone who doesn´t like you, that thinks that you should not act like you are, and that at any given time, would want you to shut up.

"I am not goint to do it, I am embarrassed" it is also used to avoid problems and uncomfortable situations. So today work in something that embarrases you.

If you are scared of speaking in public, tell a history to 5 people at the same time, increase the number of people in the following weeks. No matter what you say, just increase it.

If you panic to see that people look at you when you are dancing, do it in front of everyone you can. I have seen a boy dancing on the subway fatal five times in different stations and wagons. The guy goes with his headphones and he is a mess. Everyone looks at him, and I've never seen without a smile on his face.

Why is this challenge worth doing? What do I get out of it?

Long ago, I discovered that there is an incredible relationship between embarrassment and self confidence. The more of the first one the less of the other. And since I started to forget that I have shame I have done much better in life. I started with a personal blog, and look! Now I have a book that has been translated into Chinese and may be translated into more languages. I have also 6 more books to come plus several mobile apps and 2 online projects.

Don´t be afraid of being embarrassed. It can take you higher.

Chapter 4. Write a letter to one of your friends. Right now

Right now means right now, don´t wait any longer. Well just finish reading this chapter. You can begin writing it in a piece of paper, a receipt or in your phone. Afterwards make it pretty.

Dont write it on your computer and then print it. You can´t either dictate it or ask for help.

Hand write a letter to whoever you want. Easier to someone you already know the address. You can also deliver it personally.

Why is this challenge worth doing? What do I get out of it?

We live surrounded by machines, and we have forgotten what it was to:

1. Hand write a letter

2. Have to go and buy stamps

3. Look for a postbox

4. Finding out the address of that person

And currently a strange thing to do:

1. Waiting

Do something different

> 2. Not knowing if it has been read, if you will get an
>   answer...

Basically: we are not used to this anymore, and from every unknown situation we learn something. It is this book premise, and when you send out that letter you will be in that state of uncertainty that we had before internet existed.

Chapter 5. Good morning, what has been my mistake?

Today's exercise will focus on the admission of an irrefutable fact: you are not perfect. Maybe you are trying to be perfect by reading this book, or maybe I you are just doing it for fun. I would do the second.

The way to admit this is as follows: look for feedback. Go to the office and send a private email to each of your colleagues if you want to. Although I do not advise this and I would rather do it face to face sure there will be a shy fellow who does not know what to say, and thinks that you have put him in a compromise and needs some distance to communicate honestly.

It is important that leaders and people who report to us participate. Do the same at home. I guess at home you won´t need an email.

Write down everything. And do not ever make those mistakes again (if they are). Maybe its just a small characteristic of your personality that annoys people, in which case we can always adapt to others. Such as avoiding the black humor jokes about people with cancer in front of someone who lost a family member to it. If you don´t ask you may think "Wow, this idiot doesn´t like me and doesn´t laugh at my jokes.".

Why is this challenge worth doing? What do I get out of it?

As I started earlier: you are not perfect, nor the center of the world. You're just one more. Want to stand out of the crowd? Don´t make the same mistakes again. That will make you improve yourself.

Just getting to know that your teammates have an opinion of you should be enough to improve. But if you find out where your mistakes are, dont think about it and improve yourself.

I advise you to do it one by one. As weekly mini-challenges. That means maybe you should spend more time with this challenge before jumping to the next one. Surely, you may overlap this one with another.

Chapter 6. Create a system of confusion

Some time ago I raised a problem that I was never solved: the need to communicate information without the informant knew if it has been read or not, and in which all participants (transmitter-receiver) lose control of the situation, after sending the message.

By accident I came across an odd warning system (to call it somehow). What it does is the following. We have the following roles:

1. You
2. Person the message is directed to
3. Person that helps

Instructions are given to a third party (Person who helps) to hide an envelope that you have written in a place where the person to whom it is addressed can locate by chance. It is important that the place has a low key transit but not any. For example, the summer clothes closet if you are a girl or the cleaning products closet if you're a guy.

You, as creator of the envelope, once delivered you have no control over the information within. That is, you can not edit it. Nor you have the power to deliver the envelope. This is not like a classic letter, and therefore the delivery time will depend on where the person is located.

Even so, whether that person has opened it or not, you will not know if he has unless that person tell you. Asking is useless, since he may not even know of the existence of the letter. And you have no idea where it is, you can not help him

Do something different

to find it.

It is, without doubt, a whole system of confusion. The delivery or reception can occur shortly after placing the envelope, maybe later or never be found.

Why is this challenge worth doing? What do I get out of it?

The truth is that this idea came to me after reading about the experiment of Schrödinger's cat, and because of necessity I might say. Don´t expect it to come to your mind, design a new one.

This requires not only strategy, but an ability to foresee consequences. And, like any skill, practice will make you dominate it in the future.

Chapter 7. Forward and back in time

I admit it, I like the time. Also talking about it. I want to introduce you to a small story I wrote back in time and I wanted to edit it for this book. Don't worry; it won't take too much. I'll follow you to the end again.

"We are shaking. Pulling out from each other as we hug we left the with a quiescence of emotions"

I hear the crash of the dry wood from the spiral staircase and each dust particle falling of the stair at her steps. With her walk, her breath is worse, weaker, farther. The ladder is made by complaining piano keys because of its antiquity, weeping from each stride while they walk away.

Hearing my own heartbeat, it slows down as her steps go further. Still going up getting, we both falling apart from each other in the forced spiral that some architect designed with decorated with dyed colors.

The railing weeps, even the walls cry at my weight when I climb up with all my strength. Finally I get to the last floor, moaning with tears in my eyes. I look down to the hole in the middle of the staircase, sad immerse into the darkness while I see her crossing the hall in the first floor.

A need to scream out loud scratches my throat drowning the screaming and fading into a whispered howl that falls floating in the air going nowhere. And she's still walking away.

With a shudder I leave the cold metallic there when I see her disappearing, and I move forward into the apartment. I hear the principal door closing before mine, just one moment after the light in the hall turns off.

Time stops and became to its normal rhythm spinning around itself, flowing forward again: to the future. A hysterical call woke me up from my dream by her side, making it real. I opened the door for her in the apartment entrance and immediately I went out to my floor hall. Not closing my door, down I hear hers opening in the distance, five floors under mine. The staircase's light turns on.

A strong need to scream her name escapes in a sigh when I remember it's dawn. Hurrying, I swing on the metallic railing so I can see the illuminated staircase. I walk down to the fourth floor panting with watering eyes. The ladder claps to each one of my steps, even the walls cry with excitement while I keep walking my way down.

Still going down in the staircase, getting closer to her, both getting closer to each other spinning into a circle now with a romantic touch while I walk down to meet her.

The only complaining to the architect is this twisted staircase around itself in a way far from the center, in my opinion, making infinite the journey downstairs. I hear my own heart beat accelerating to the rhythm of her steps getting closer.

Her breathing sounds better with every step, more clear. The staircase made by piano keys of enthusiasm and vitality that laugh at her feet as they approach. I hear the crash of the wood from the spiral staircase and each dust particle falling while she walks.

We reached each other falling into a hug with a quiescence of emotions. We shook."

(End of story)

Probably you didn't realize there are staircases that actually make that sound, they crash.

If you take another look to the narration, it has the next structure: first there's action, something happens; then the opposite. Turning the tense in a specific part of the story. Have you ever thought what would happen if you change the tense of some verbs in a precise part of your text?

At this time, I write, it seems to click the button that appears to clear the computer.

So what is this exercise for? What do I win with that?

In the book I repeat several times about seeing things with other perspective, that will help you in your life because we all need to improve our divergent thoughts.

How would I leave it apart?

There's always a problem where you have to count on time. Maybe it's the most important factor.

- It can't be controlled.
- It won't stop.
- It costs a lot of money.

Time is probably the most important element we work with in our entire life. I invite to put in your time in every situation you get into today as an exercise. The truck's delivered load would be the truck's shipment, water will be back to the tap and food will be preserve again in its original packs. Many inventions were thought from a divergent way of doing things and working on this is recommended to appreciate our nature further than a straight sight as humans are used to.

Chapter 8. Create a Schedule. Break it all the time

We all live with a work and duties schedule. We will say that (for obvious reasons) we must fulfill it to the letter. As an example we will say that we want to get paid by end of the month. But then there is a free time schedule, aspirations, personal improvement, etc. Within that we can find activities such as learning English, going to the gym, finding time to read a book,...

We all know what happens with this type of schedule. In the end we do nothing, we feel bad, and just throwing away the piece of paper we sticked to the refrigerator. I also, and incidentally, take some chocolate. Mine is a strong will.

Well, forget the schedule and planning. Write or print a squared sheet each with a week of the year. For example, "Week 1, January 1 to January 7." Leave enough space to write in the boxes.

Now, above every one of them write down vertically all those activities that you won´t go to:

      1. Language lessons
      2. Gym
      3. Reading
      4. ...
And instead of having a strict schedule, make it a "flexible Schedule".

What the hell is this? This is a schedule in which you write down lines the invested hours (or number of times) you have spent doing an activity. So, every week, you will "acumulate lines" and you'll see if you're consistent or not. It is not about going every Monday and Wednesday to the gym, but, come Sunday, we went a couple of times at some point during the week.

To put several examples, I wake up at about eight o'clock most days. The first thing I do is having a shower and then breakfast. Afterwards I read my emails and answer the outstanding ones. That leads to 9.30. For the next three hours I study, to get it out of the way, and then finally 1 hour before lunchtime I write my daily post. Just after lunch I go to the gym, and by 4.30 I have finished all the "mandatory" self activities.

So I add those activities to my Wall Schedule. By the end of the month I should have studied at least 28 days, gone to the gym 20 days and written the book 15 or more. Otherwise, I expect a hard challenge month to recover.

Why is this challenge worth doing? What do I get out of it?

When within a month you pick the first four or five weeks, then you will realize what has been achieved. Probably nothing, but I am sure you have done something. Ok, now try to improve those goals. Do not make them too complex, it is not about counting the minutes you´ve been on your bike, but to acquire a habit in cycling (for example).

We usually get schedules that often for verifiable excuses or reasons can not be kept. Turn over the conventional schedule and work with a flexible and cumulative schedule.

Chapter 9. Write an essay

Do you remember when you were young and the literature teacher asked you (insitently) to write a free topic essay?

Of course my writing was always about the space, aliens or dinosaurs, truck-dinosaurs, truck-aliens, and sometimes even of events that happened in real life. Funny stuff, you know.

How long has it been since you last wrote an essay? How long has it been since you last sat down for 2 hours to write an essay? Don´t write it just for yourself but also for somebody that will analyze its structure.

It is totally up to you the topic of the essay. Maybe an essay about how beautiful the countryside is, or a conversation between 2 people.

Most of the time we have no idea of what we want in life, but this point wants to address something closer to us. Have you ever thought "I want to talk about this" and done it?

I don´t mean to talk in front of your friends at the bar, I know you're capable of that, even with a mouthful of nachos and talking way louder than your friends while you lengthen your arms in a strategic position that brings you closer to the nachos and makes your friends shut up at once.

I mean sitting quietly in front of a blank page (be careful, it can very scary) and typing what you want to tell the world correctly so anyone that reads it understands it. Try it.

What do you want to talk about ? Realizing that fact not

only will let you know more about yourself, but will let you target your conversations where you want them, and not where they others want.

Everyone has a hobby. There is people, for example, that likes Moto GP You can stay hours watching in front of the screen watching each of them overtaking the other. Yet, not withstanding a technical talk on bikes.

Knowing what we want helps us to make better decisions. You may not have any idea of what to tell. In that case I always advise reading the incongruities of "SEMI-AUTOMATIC WRITING, LET´S SAY 01", an essay by @pobrebicho (twitter account) that always makes me feel better when writing. It is a small paragraph with nonsense words, such as Lewis Carrol´s Hatta.

Chapter 10. Change the order of the words

Spanish is one of the most difficult languages to learn. Among other reasons because we do whatever we want with it and the "Real Academia de la Lengua" (Royal Academy of Spanish as a language) allows us to do it. As this is an English translation I will try to explain this as simple as I can.

In Spanish we use something called "double denial" in sentences. This means we can use don´t and nothing in the same sentence. We write (literaly translated) "In this room there are not noone". This sentence doesn´t make any sense in English. It doesn´t even make any sense in Spanish either, but that doesn´t stop us from using it. In Spanish we would use that sentence to say "There is noone in the room", so to say that a room is empty we say that "nobody" is "not there".

Another example is the word "inflamable" (flammable in English). In Spanish we have put to the word "flamable" the prefix "in-" (which is a denial). So "inflamable" should mean that the object can´t burn. But the meaning in reality is that it can burn and explode.

Have you ever heard the expression " I´m happy because of you"? Probably not, and it´s such a shame, because changing the meaning of the words can make you smile, look online for "You rock, you rule" if you have never seen it.

"This is the last time I fall in love with you" (In Spanish this is an ultimatum).

Why is this challenge worth doing? What do I get out of it?

Do you think you can give a word or a sentence a different use of the current one?

It is true that it´s possible you may confuse people, but after a "click" their mind and yours will change. Now it´s your turn to create one sentence where the meaning of a word is altered by the rest of the contents of the sentence.

Chapter 11. Find a movie you don´t like. Now watch it

Yes, I know, who would want to watch a movie you know you will not like? It doesn´t seem to be a very intelligent thing to do if you want to have a good time. At first glance it may seem stupid to watch a movie or read a book that you know you will not like, why bother to finish it if you know you don´t like it? But of course, you must remember that the purpose of this book is not to spend a good time. It is for you to learn. If you want, afterwards you can go and watch a movie you like. As Sergio Fernández (pensamientopositivo.org) says, he reads a "learning book" once a week. And also besides that he reads about other topics.

In my case it´s about warlike or historical movies. They bore me to death. When I watch them it seems that nothing has happened during the whole movie. Despite my feelings about them I always watch at least once a year one of them.

That means that, for 3 or 4 hours a year (maybe many more), I am bored to death in front of the computer. In fact, the other day I went with a friend to watch a movie whose main actor has screwed up for me all the movies I have watched where he was acting. Why did I go? Why have I paid for something that I knew I wouldn´t like?

To answer this I will give another example. How many times have you had fun in class? An hour out of ten? Out of twenty? And yet, you will be with me, that those other many hours of boredom and lethargy have helped you at some point. Whether because of the knowledge you got or because you opened up your mind.

But a miracle can always happen. How do you know that five minutes after you start you will not love it? You don´t know, you'll have to start watching it.

Why is this challenge worth doing? What do I get out of it?

Giving a chance to a genre that you don´t like (at first). I have to say that I don´t usually like westerns movies, so it took me years to see a movie called Serenity (listed as futuristic western) and now is a film that I could watch again and again and has opened my eyes a lot . Not particularly a great movie, I have to even say that this is a film that closes a series that wasn´t even successful. But it's different, and I found it by mistake.

Giving a second (or twentieth) chance to an actor, director or genre will never go against you. On the contrary, it will greatly expand your world.

Most likely you are right, and if from the beginning you feel you won´t like something, at the end that might be true. But I am one of those that believes that you can learn something from everything. And in every movie, Sharknado included, there is at least one interesting sentence.

Chapter 12. Imaginary world workshops. Invent a world, then develop it

Imagine a crazy condition. The more absurd that you are able to imagine. For example: Imagine that suddenly everyone in the world loses the right foot. I am not talking about a mega multiple accident or an attack. Simply all right foot disappear overnight, similar to the mental experiment that Alan Weisman makes on "The World Without Us," a world where humans simply disappear.

Do you have your example already?

Start working on it. Wonder how we would live if it occurs. Or what would change in the world. Following my example:

Would the prosthesis or crutches be improved? Would we change the way we manufacture shoes? And the pedals in cars? Is there anyone who would benefit from this situation? How long will it be on the news? What fears will it awake? How would it change our way thinking?

Put your brain and your deductive techniques to work for your absurd condition. We all know what happens when you release an egg and it hits the ground, but how many people would know what would happen if everyone in the world forgot how to read or how to spell? Did someone have thought of it? Do it. Try to imagine solutions for imposible to imagine situations.

Why is this challenge worth doing? What do I get out of it?

Exercise your mind. Deductive reasoning is a basic tool for everyday life. Anticipating situations as a result of something is very useful in day to day life. For example: You're in the car and you see announced an accident on a route you usually take to go home. What do you do? How does the accident affect the dynamics of all the surrounding streets? Is it worth a detour or is it preferable to stay in the car listening to music a couple of minutes with the engine off?

Reasoning and deducting alternative scenarios helps us to strengthen these tools to ask questions and increase our responsiveness. A fun exercise is to raise this to a friend, and see the differences in our deductions and questions. Will you see a world emerged from a absurd condition in the same way?

It´s been a while since I practice this and not long ago I have introduced this Imaginary Worlds Workshop on my blog, so you can check out for ideas. Or just enjoy reading them. Unfortunately I have not had time to write about the already sixty ideas that have been sent to me by readers, among which are cases like that everyone is born with the heart outside the chest or cellulose has not already been processed as paper.

You can always enter www.pensamientolateral.org and propose some hypothesis. You will find that there are some other stories about it, but less than I would want. Alan Weisman has done well.

Chapter 13. Write down a plan to rule the world.

I know, it sounds silly. In fact, it is nonsense. But it is not a useless nonsense writing, but spending hours reading other plans for world domination is (some of them are funny I admit it). Writing them is a mental challenge, and that is what we care about.

What is a plan of world domination and where can I document myself?

Frikipedia (Spanish website, a humor wikipedia) began as a side project to Wikipedia (prestigious online encyclopedia). But everything is in humor, it has place to everyone that knows how to write. You can edit it at any time.

A plan to rule the world is a strategy (extremely absurd) of how to become master of the world. There's even one "Freak Guide of How to rule the world" in which hundreds of plans are exposed Quite an achievement for lateral thinking and collective writing.

How is a plan for world domination written? Each plan has the following structure:

Main Storyline. Here a couple of lines of how you intend to achieve this global domination are written. An example (the BN Plan) would be: You get a taco stall (food), put in front of the white house, with a huge sign that reads "PRESIDENT EATS FREE TACOS". Then you poison the meat, and when the president eats them, dies. Then you just need cross the street and raise yourself as the new president and master of the world (Hint: put on his clothes).

Pros: arguments for a crazy theory. For example, continuing with the previous case: The President can´t resit to some good free tacos and on top of that you don´t have to walk too far away, it´s just across the road.

Cons: is not that simple. Even the most absurd plans for world domination must have cons. The example is: Do you think it is so easy to circumvent the security of the White House? In addition, before the president eats there, the bodyguards will punch you because you've placed an illegal business in front of the White House (and even more if they find out that the tacos are poisonous).

Do you think you could write one? I don´t take a "Bah, is nonsense." Try it, and challenge your friends.

Why is this challenge worth doing? What do I get out of it?

They say you are born with imagination or without it. I disagree perpendicular to this statement (not 180 degrees). And it helps to have imagination, but it is not everything. Like any skill, it can be trained. Who knows? Just after writing a few plans for world domination you could write and publish a book like this one. Or not.

Chapter 14. Be careful with backhand stroke

A long time ago there was a pretty weird guy named Isaac. This guy said (and so far has been right) when you exert force on to one type of system, it tends to counteract it to remain as it was.

That is, the systems do not want to change. And I have bad news for you, businesses, families, individuals, are all systems. Even your dog is a system. And if he cans he won´t do anything but eat and shit all his life.

So what can be expected is that if you do something outside the normal behavior line (something I'm continually trying with this book) you must wait a setback by everything around you.

Do you want to change from A to B? You'll meet many people who will tell you:

1. You are crazy.

2. You do not know what you are doing.

3. You're wrong.

4. You don´t live in the real world.

So now what we do is get out of the normal line of behavior. I'm talking about going up the stairs five floors. Organize your desktop in a different way each day, park further away from work to walk a little. Something that is different from what you usually every day.

Why is this challenge worth doing? What do I get out of it?

I keep telling you to challenge yourself, to do something unexpected, to leave your comfort zone, embarrassment or whatever you call it and get to do something you will feel proud of. You should know in advance that, now, once you do it the world will want to go against you.

Enemies you didn't have will show up, some people will look at you weirdly, you'll probably discover who supports you really and who doesn't.

A lot of different circumstances may happen, but you have to know that if you work to change, change will happen. And some of them might not be pleased with that.

Chapter 15. Counting stars. A matter of trust

"Tell a man there are 400 billion stars and he'll believe you. Tell him the wall has fresh paint and he will touch it."

What can we say about this except that it is a great truth? I do not know who said this. Just went a while and I've internalized as part of the popular knowledge or I don´t remember the origin.

If someone says "this smells funny" by necessity, another nose while smell it to confirm that information. I am the first one to do it.

Why don´t we trust information given by someone else´s senses and have to check it anyway? By the way, if someone wanted to count stars it´s my fault, the chapter title can be misleading. But you can go out of town any night and check it.

We systematically check all the information we can, even knowing that the source is reliable. This is the syndrome experienced by mothers when they ask for our homework. They have to see it as if it was OCD or any other mental illness.

But how much time do we lose a day checking verified information?

The challenge today is to believe. Believe everything you are told. Well, if it is April´s Fools to the next chapter, just in case.

Why is this challenge worth doing? What do I get out of it?

If you have felt identified, congratulations! You're a control freak. Write me an email and we can build an organization. I'm serious. People like us need to learn to let go and trust other people. You will realize that, after a day, a week, a month you will not constantly check all information that passes through your hands.

Chapter 16 On taking it all too seriously

Ok, people may say I don´t take life too seriously, that I'm always smiling and I make jokes are not relevant to that particular moment all the time. But as Elbert Hubbard said, "Do not take life too seriously. You will never get out of it alive."

You know what is to be typing on the computer and the lights go out, losing everything you wrote?

Here you can find two possible behaviours:

1. Exploding literally like a bomb, swear and take down all your office´s furniture.

2. Turn on the computer, schedule a backup every 5 minutes and start again.

Believe me, it has happened to me more times than I'm willing to admit, and every single time by blood has boiled, and I´ve had an increased urge to kill. With that I learned that we have so much energy inside, but it only seems to be released as swears and insults, usually against poor guys who have no guilt.

The next time you are angry and you want heads to roll, try to calm down and transform all that energy into work. Or go to the gym.

"The report has been deleted? You'll see ... I will now do it better"

Why is this challenge worth doing? What do I get out of it?

It is very difficult to realize our mistakes, but occasionally something can help us find them. Next time laugh about it and learn from the mistake. I know that if something similar happened yesterday you now want to hit me with all your strength. I understand it perfectly. I want to strike you all sometimes.

Chapter 17 Chinese dishes (juggling sing) and the importance of delegating

This challenge can be complex, so you'll have to read it slowly.

Sometimes both personal and in the business world, we are overwhelmed with activities that take us the whole day. Who has not ever thought that a day has not enough hours?

Life is a Chinese dishes game. It is better to decide which one is going to fall. Because believe me, at least one is going to fall. That´s it. Everything will not be perfect, because no matter how hard you try in life there are always variables that simply are beyond your control.

Ideally (if you can) is to transfer that responsibility to another person or business you trust, and, of course, in which you can delegate without any problem. We all know colleagues who show up and give you their work because they just simply don´t want to finish it.

So you should ask yourself the following questions:

What am I good at? What activity is easy for me to do?

First of all, be clear that you will not know how good you are in any position until do it for a while.

If you're good at something is highly recommended that you do it because it will better than letting someone with less ability do it. However you can always raise the problem of lack of time, in which case you must train someone.

Do not skimp on training times, in some companies and even entire industries training of workers is the only R&D that can be performed.

We all have skills and abilities, however, discover what you are good at or recognize the things you do best requires a process of self-analysis, you can even get help with some career guidance test, but nothing like experience.

Sometimes our workers can see the delegation of a task as more work. Let´s make it clear that meeting the working hours and a respecting a good salary, what we want to show is that we believe that person is great for the role. Otherwise, we would have given it to someone else. Transmitting this is very important for the worker to know the reasons for the new responsibility and not tackle it as a burden. And the same is true at home.

Not long ago, I was having lunch with a friend and we were speaking about the house work her nephew had to do. The day before he had prepared all the ingredients to make a cookie dough, and then had cleaned the table. He is four years and, besides that, is in charge of keeping his room tidy, so he can choose his birthday present plus a dessert of his choice once a week.

Something in what you are disastrous at?

Again several options: you can have a give the task to someone else or take the opportunity to learn from it. If you choose the latter not underestimate to spend more hours in the office. Spending more hours learning will never go against you. Never.

Learning will always give you points in life. Teaching even more.

Is it really important to do this now?

Having a way to categorize the importance or the time of the projects is as vital as knowing what projects to invest in. We will have to finish first what is really urgent. What under no circumstances can be done tomorrow? And this leads to the following:

Do not leave for tomorrow what can be done today

This saying that is in our hearts and we don´t usually follow may be even wrong. Ideally do today what can´t be done tomorrow, or what is more urgent. Leave for tomorrow all tasks you want, whenever you are able to do them the next day. Today have fun ... if you can.

This, of course, is a double-edged sword, it may be useless to have two full work days if you're not able to focus. Maybe it's better to have a two hour day and the next one a twelve hour.

Learn to value yourself and your team. Occasionally, a "let's all grab a coffee" can save a workweek.

Marcos Martínez @euklidiadas

We are all saturated, what do we do?

How many times have we seen the whole department overwhelmed? For weeks the Project has been very stressful, delivering quantity but not quality. Stress is all over the place and mood is not the highest.

This, of course, affects the quality and speed of work. And it will get worse.

Find solutions outside is ok, although outsourcing or out-tasking in many companies is seen as not accepted, and even, by some workers as an insult to their productive capacity. If so the focus has to be similar to "we are so good that the orders are simply beyond our capacity and we need help from outside."

Delegating responsibility for outsourcing to a any of those technicians will not only get their collaboration, but their understanding as middle management. In addition to be contributing to their training by giving them more responsibility.

"We can't achieve this". Saying no to a client

After considering joining a project or extending it we realize that we can't achieve it. Also we could not find a any outsourcing help that we deem reliable or which price will give profit. That is, if we take another customer our Chinese dishes will fall.

In this case, we should not be afraid to turn down a job making it clear to the client the reasons why you can not do it. Customers are composed of human people, and we all like honesty. Excuses can damage our image.

Do something different

Let's just say no to work, clarifying that we would love to meet their needs next time, but right now the company is working on other projects it has already committed. This would leave our reputation intact to be considered for the next project.

Why is this challenge worth doing? What do I get out of it?

This is one of the most complex exercises because it has hundreds of possible permutations. Hence its length. You may have people reporting into you and don´t know what this is all about. But try looking at it from the perspective of which someone that is below, if you're above. Don´t you wish you could depend somewhat on his criteria? Give him some of the power that you are unable to drive?

As I said before, and as anticipated at the beginning of the book, this is not only applicable in the field of work or business, but on a day to day basis we must decide which tasks can be performed, in which ones to ask for help is needed and which ones we can´t achieve.

Chapter 18 From home to work and from work to home

If you are moderately lucky,or you work a lot, you have a job. I know you don´t like it, are disgusted and hate it. Every day you will get into the office already thinking when will you leave. Plus you hate your boss and your boss's boss, and you wonder if the police will notice axes on their backs. In answer to your question: yes, it is very likely, currently the police has the coolest techniques to catch you.

For the less fortunate (those who are not working), I'm sure there is a certain route you follow.

if possible, so that we lose an infinity of intermediate points that could be seen. I'm not talking about going to work around the other side of town, but usually we tend to get from point A to point B by drawing a straight line occasionally frequent these roads Google Maps says will take you 1 more minute.

There is a popular saying that goes "If you expect the same results don´t do always the same." Some guy called Albert say so, I believe. So I recommend follow those alternative paths.

Do you normally walk? Find a park near your route and go through it. I know, it is possible that, due to the distance to work, you can not walk or cycle. But think that if it takes you an hour or less by bike, there is no justification for not doing so.

Do you drive to the office? Try to get another traffic jam somewhere else in the city.

Do something different

Of course begin this game when you are coming back from the office because it might take you longer. Exit the subway at different stops, change at different places. Change driving to commuting. New experiences involve new thoughts and ideas.

Why is this challenge worth doing? What do I get out of it?

You know those times when a friend tells you that he has found great restaurant? Or who has seen an offer that you haven´t?

New bars, new places to walk around, maybe a shorter (or more enjoyable) path. If you do not change your route, you will always see the same opening or closing stores, the same streets and the same people.

If you can also move cycling or walking, you save on gym and save on gasoline.

And, of course, you will receive stimuli other than the usual, obtaining also different ideas.

Chapter 19 The pen that was useless to write with

Imagine you buy something. For example a pen, but maybe a glass, a fan or a pack of 500 sheets... And now imagine that you can not use it for what it is supposed to. It is forbidden, or broken, I do not care. Anyway, you can not use it as it´s meant to. You are required to give it different use. That is your challenge today.

"How the heck can I use a pen that can´t write?" I wondered a while.

When I started this challenge I looked around and found a box of colored pencils that I've probably dragged from primary school without giving them any use. However, reform after reform, the pens are dragged out of a drawer to another without much sense just to leave them there for a while before changing the contents of the drawer.

They are the classical wooden pencils. And now, in addition, they are my modem cooling system. My modem is very hot at the base, so I've built a small tower to raise it and allow the heated air to go out naturally.

Why is this challenge worth doing? What do I get out of it?

Have you ever played one of those games that require lateral thinking to be solved? Have you ever wondered if there is any training for it? This exercise is one of the few classic exercises documented as enhancement of lateral thinking.

For two years I worked in an office where, with some cardboard boxes, I made some shelves for paperwork. They ended up being as big as cupboard. And even my teammates gave him the nickname "Bethlehem", because one of them, crammed with junk, had similarities with the Nativity.

Use your mind to find other use for objects. But please, disposable, we don´t want to take your car apart.

Chapter 20 Don´t go the shortcuts, find tools and work hard

We are so used to search shortcuts that the work we produce may be, inconsistent, incomplete and even wrong.

Today we will make a small analysis exercise. Every time you fill out a form, document, each time you open an Excel file ask yourself: Is this the best way to do this?

I come from the world of telecommunications. The definition of the world would be something like: now, fast, don´t worry about tomorrow´s tasks, deliver it, then go to the next thing.

Unfortunately, a lack of inventory of a mobile group for the past five or ten years has meant that today prices are not set correctly, but below the profit in some cases, the timeframe is literally impossible and that the disorder and confusion are everyday´s issues. It's no secret that I left the telecommunications sector in a hospital box with a diagnosis of anxiety because of the atmosphere of chaos and disorder that ruled the company.

So ask yourself: Does what I do help? Is there any other way to do it? Will I be able to use it next year if I do it this way or will I have to do it again? If I work another minute in each document, I'll end up saving time after a year because I won´t rewrite everything twice?

Why is this challenge worth doing? What do I get out of it?

Companies look for living people with initiative. Someone who saves thousands per year and thousands more for next year is a great asset, and they will keep him. I'm talking about serious, obviously.

Want to make you strong in your workplace? Make everything you do a lot more efficient. And, incidentally, exercise your mind a little. Question all the procedures. Some will perfect, most of them can be improved, and others useless and can be recycled somehow.

Chapter 21. Invent words

The previously mentioned Royal Academy of Spanish Language hasn´t yet included in its dictionary the word "trigonometry" even though it is thousands of years old. Despite that in 2012 they did include words such as "geek" and "sudoku". Because of this I feel I have the right to invent words. It will be easier to get them in the dictionary if they are new it seems.

I usually invent "combwords" (combined words) to join to meanings into one word. For example:

The second dessert after dinner is called "dessercond".

"Emojinary", the dictionary of emojis.

Who will tell me that they wont be used in the near future? And I am not the only one. If you think it twice, words that you are currently using were invented at some point in time. Why not you being the next one?

Why is this challenge worth doing? What do I get out of it?

We are usually lazy. The less the better. And this also applies to the brain. When was the last time you solved a puzzle? And the last time you solved a mind game? With this game you will make your mind work harder.

Quickly, come on! Invent a game. Now!

Chapter 22 Absurdity, imagination par excellence

Long ago, someone said: someday mankind will fly over the oceans. Probably the first thought on this was thousands of years ago. And he was labeled as crazy, it took thousands of years to prove him right.

Something not being possible today does not mean that won´t be possible (or not happen) tomorrow. The climate change alarmists began to appear in the nineteenth century. Lunatics, all was well. Until now, when it turns out that those lunatics were people who simply knew how to deduce the facts long before they were relevant.

Think that the big silly questions from some early era are what today maintains society. Imagine your grandfather was told when he was young that he was going to be able to talk with hundreds of people with a portable phone. If you were lucky he didn´t slap you, but he certainly told you to shut up.

In fact we are currently missing absurd ideas, it has been already 50 years without a new one. Are you up for the challenge?

Why is this challenge worth doing? What do I get out of it?

Having an original thought is not easy. For it to happen, all planets must be aligned, or you must have gone through a disaster or gone through a moment of absolute clarity to have your mind opened. (This challenge continues in 23 chapter)

Chapter 23 Share your absurd idea

(this is a continuation of Chapter 22)

Okay, you've discovered something that humanity has been seeking for the last hundred years. It is a revolutionary, amazing ... and very very stupid idea. It´s not enough just to stay there. Once you have discovered your absurd idea you should share it. Moreover, I accept nonsense stuff here: pensamientolateral.org.

If you think you have a shocking, funny but taboo idea, something that humanity has done wrong for thousands of years, feel free to tell it. You can also email me now, just to say hello. That may be your challenge today: write me. Or write anyone else to tell your big plans for the future. We all have big plans for the future, right?

Why is this challenge worth doing? What do I get out of it?

Somewhere in the book I talk about overcoming embarrassment. This challenge, in a way, wants to defy social awareness a Little.

If you notice every time someone does something mildly outrageous or not normal we tend to "correct him". That is, society (all of us) are our own guards and jailers. What we keep are the dangerous ideas that change in any way the reality in which we live. We don´t want to change. Fuck! You are also a system (see Chapter 14, "Beware the reverse"). But we must do, and it begins with absurd ideas.

Chapter 24 Create lies to get caught

Today I want you to do an experiment. Write on paper something like: "What I told you about my holidays was a lie". Now fold it, put it in an envelope, seal it and put it in a colleague´s jacket, purse or backpack when he doesnt look. Third step: tell him about those wonderful family holidays you´ve just had. With your three children, if you have two, two if you have three and none if you have one (for example).

Every two aspects that you tell about the holidays, one must be a lie. Moreover, you have not even had to go on vacation. Do it naturally.

Why is this challenge worth doing? What do I get out of it?

"Lying is bad" is a phrase we have heard since childhood, and even now we get angry if someone lies to us.

I have to say that the lies are classified into two types: those that are necessary and those that come out of selfishness. If you have a business and have no money for your workers but you'll have in a day, you can tell them you already have it. If you have not purchased a birthday gift tell them you have fogot it and you will give it next time you see each other.

Lies can save you from several awkward social moments, especially if you know that people well. Doing it naturally is a challenge. And is today´s challenge. By the way, the envelope is so that when you get caught and called a liar and you can demonstrate that it is an experiment. Lie!

Chapter 25 The languages issue

I don't know how to speak English (obviously, I paid that translation). Believe me I've tried to learn it. I've been to academies to tried to learn it. I have also paid teachers to come and talk to me at home. I've met people from around the world to have a coffee and for years all I watch is its native language. Also, I hear the BBC for a couple of hours every day.

My brain simply can not handle English. Some brains can't handle mathematical formalism, and some people will never understand philosophy.

I have put the issue of languages of languages for instance in what, I believe, I will not improve in my life.

And because I know my weakness is one of the points that I attack. Obviously, it's English and not Kurdish. I know I am not good at it, but at least what I learn is useful. A few months ago, I translate into English poetry of Ray Bradbury, one page daily. It is about half an hour of my time to write and understand a single page.

Today, I want you to choose a major barrier that you think you need to improve. You might be public relations manager without any computer skills for Social Media Marketing or a security guard who is not able to run half a mile without throwing up.

Why is this challenge worth doing? What do I get out of it?

We all have limitations. To deny this fact is quite absurd. You will never jump over a certain amount of inches, or you will never earn more than a certain amount of money. That's life.

But we all can force these limits to reach its maximum and leave them there as long as we can.

Learning where our limits are help us to be more objective about ourselves facing the future. So find your limits and try to move them slightly with a lot of effort.

Chapter 26 In a debate or argument, if you reach an agreement, change your opinion to discuss more

To agree, anyone whom you may ask, usually has good attributes. Agreeing makes two or more people to agree, focuses and unifies the views, generates synergies, makes fewer discussions, promotes warmth and lots of incredibly results:

- Boring;
- Complacent;
- Ambitionless;
- Bland;
- Extremely soporific;
- And sometimes the end of a conversation.

Why do we want to agree? Obviously, on important issues (such as how to run a country) it is expected to have a relatively stable system. But you are not the prime minister, nobody is going to be affected with what you say in a meal or a meeting with friends.

Since you're small you are suggested that thinking to match the 95% of people is acceptable, logical and uncomplicated. And you should fit. That is why you must like football, piercings are bad and someone as nasty as to have a tattoo can never work in banking.

Why is this challenge worth doing? What do I get out of it?

As each of these games, depends on the person. But with this game you can tell, that defending the opposite idea, those other people that think outside the box might be right. Use polemics and sophism to realize other possible points of view.

It is a way to train yourself to defend your ideas to someone. Have you ever wanted to tell your boss off but you were not capable of building a single word? Train yourself!

Chapter 27 Write short stories, help me with #TCuento

For quite a while, I write a short story on Twitter. Yes, I know, more people is also doing it. But I discovered a not used hastag much shorter than the rest of them. "#TCuento" comes (in Spanish) from the shortening of "Tweet-Story", and is the shortest hastag about short stories assigned to date. I also wanted to give a new approach to this type of communication, reduced to such writing, and show the world that small fragments of text can mean a lot. I give you an example, which is my favorite.

"Traveling back in time, he met her as she was leaving. And beyond, he introduced himself with bitter tears from past strangeness."

Time travel, love, melodrama and a situation complicated enough needed to be drawn before capturing the whole concept. You see, something incredibly brief can tell a complex story.

Why is this challenge worth doing? What do I get out of it?

Writing a #TCuento may seem easy at first, but when you have fifty becomes a challenge every day, a challenge that requires five minutes of concentration: what do you want to tell, how do you want to tell it, and most difficult, sacrifice it to fit in a Tweet and be meaningful at the same time. It is a creating and perseverance exercise. One demanding enough to be frustrating at times.

Chapter 28 Win your audience with a game

This book is the best example: a manual on how to open the mind with challenges, games or personal missions that you set yourself and that hundreds of people may thank me at some time. At least, I hope so. I take this opportunity to tell you that this is a good time to email me and tell me what do you think about the book and what have you learned:

Creating a game is relatively simple: you need a goal, a couple of participants and rules for both reach that goal.

Feel like creating as I have done?

Why is this challenge worth doing? What do I get out of it?

I believe that creating is the hardest thing I've ever done in my life, and this book is my personal challenge. When you set yourself a goal, you learn from it. When you share it, everybody learns.

You can create a game in your next dinner with friends, taking a break at work, or in class, or when you get home with your flatmates. Furthermore, if you add a scoring system, achievements, and small team accomplishments you will have a great product and attentive audience.

Chapter 29. Argue with yourself

Don´t be fooled, your greatest enemy is not your boss, or that guy that doesn´t like you. Your greatest enemy is yourself. All barriers and difficulties that arise in your life are conditioned by what you think you can or can´t do. Why don´t you argue with yourself a Little?

The problem: How do I argue against myself? What do I have to do to listen to myself?

Do the following when you have an idea. Such as something to improve your office or your work: write it in a text editor, write it down as if you were talking about it with your boss. Sell it the best you can. Then close the paper and put a reminder in a few days. Maybe a week.

When you open it, read it as if that coworker you hate (can be also your brother in law) was explaining it to you. You can even put ridiculous voices to mock him. But now your role is that of your boss. What would you say to that employee that´s making you waste your time? Change something in the office? But everything works. Also, the idea is not as good.

Argue with yourself. Use different roles for a fictitious conversation with yourself.

Why is this challenge worth doing? What do I get out of it?

Usually we see everything from a single perspective (ours) without thinking of everyone else´s. This exercise allows you to see the faults you usually have when suggesting an idea, or when speaking to your boss. This exercise helps you to position yourself in a more neutral point, and see the situation in perspective.

Most likely something that helps you might disturb your colleague or might even make his work more difficult. You will gain a new perspective when you are able to position yourself in either roles.

Chapter 30: The victim. The whole world is against you

How many times have we seen our friends and family complaining about something? Or worse, how many times do we do it?

- My job sucks;
- I don´t have time to go to the gym;
- I want a change of environment but they don´t let me do it;
- ...

Okay, now back off a little. Try looking at the problem with some perspective. But note something very important: no one will give you anything for free.

In our frustration we often see the source of our failure to external factors. This happens sometimes, but always?

Let's see what is the latest thing you have failed in? Now analyze it: How much of that mistake is yours? Analyze what went wrong, why, how much do you have to blame yourself, how much others may be blamed for, how would you have acted now you know what had happened.

Why is this challenge worth doing? What do I get out of it?

Being able to take a couple of steps back gives us a perspective that we did not have before. With this exercise we can not only see our mistakes, but we can correct them in most cases. Besides seeing the future inconveniences.

Chapter 31 Congratulations, you have just got the project you wanted!

All of us, along our work and personal life, we hope. We hope to get our hands on the perfect job, the perfect house, the perfect couple.

And, while we wait, we miss many opportunities that are right in front of our eyes, thinking that the garden is always greener on other side without really enjoying what we have, and that only needs watering.

Today is your lucky day. I'm going to ask you a favor. It´s a favor because it is actually very complex. Easy concept but terribly difficult (not complex) execution.

I will now ask you to act like what you have has been chosen just by you. Another way to approach it is that it is the last day of your life, but I´d rather think positive.

This concept is not new to me nor I invented it, has to do with the "areté" (which is a rather complicated ancient Greek concept). If we can define in a simple way, areté could say that it is the pursuit of excellence in all the arts and situations.

For example: eat as if it was your last meal, do your job to get promoted tomorrow.

A more current term would be "giving 120% all the time in every situation."

Why is this challenge worth doing? What do I get out of it?

Continuous use of this technique not only will make you happier. It will also crush your spirits and make you excellent. You will achieve your goals, but beware of the fatigue.

Definitely fighting is good, but let's keep effort to 95% in the long term. I mean always get up on the tube even if the person is your same age and has no mobility problems.

Chapter 32 Choose random words in the dictionary

Grab a dictionary or encyclopedia. Open it by any page at random. In the unlikely event that your house does not have one of the hundreds of millions of encyclopedias that were sold during the 90's, you can always enter http://www.listofrandomwords.com/ and choose random words generator.

Choose a few at random. One, two, three, four, ... the more you choose the more complicated the challenge will be. And now the challenge begins: you have to use those words in a period of one week. And it is very likely that you on´t know how to use them in a conversation.

If it is usually difficult to have common theme in a conversation, you'll see how funny is to try with strange words. Let´s see in what context you use "adscititous", "bardolatry" or "bezoar". And therein lies the challenge.

Why is this challenge worth doing? What do I get out of it?

Defending our ideas is probably one of the most complicated aspects of our lives. How do I translate what I have in mind so as to be able to convince the person that I have with me? Have you ever wondered why people know how to sell you anything?

Can you be trained? I certainly was. Try these random words. If you succeed, what will you not be able to bring up in a conversation?

Tickle your brain and divert the conversation to your words. Although you'll have to work a little at first it will be helpful to make the leap from "conversation" to "what I want to talk about today." Because it's not the same. Do you ever wonder why there is people who knows how to direct talks?

Chapter 33 Mental Stop

Have you ever read that that patience science mother? Well that's a lie. Science´s mother is proof, not silly staring at a wall.

This is, however, what I will ask you to do today. Well, you can choose to look at a wall, a chair, a park, a window, etc.

Stay a while staring what you want to stare at. You can´t use electronic devices, televisions or similar. Neither a group of people nearby. If there is people, it has to be far away. You have to observe without thinking.

Today we will do nothing for half an hour. You may not think that you have the time, but you can take it out right after work, or break, maybe after dinner.

We'll let the mind wander, (it is very difficult to leave the mind empty unless you're a dead weasel). But somehow disconnect.

Why is this challenge worth doing? What do I get out of it?

We all need our space, but between us and that precious time: study, work, kids, various obligations, everyday problems, etc.

What can we do to not become totally crazy? Not much, but there´s something we can do.

Have you ever been sitting by the fireplace? Turns out we've been doing for thousands of years to disconnect the mind. There must be a reason to do it. As you may not probably have a fireplace in your house you may have to settle with a beautiful scenery. Or go buy a DVD recording of a fireplace (it really exists).

Personally this is the most difficult challenge that I have because my mind does not want to stop, especially if there is no stimulus. But ninety percent of my posts have come from these periods of peace.

Chapter 34 Shameless

When we were at high school my classmates I played a game in class. I must say that it was not a game proposed by the teacher, but literally was played during the "class". I put class in quotes because that subject was called Study and the teacher who gave us that class had the lowest IQ and zero aspirations. That was his job: observe. I still do not understand how he could stand that. I guess he didn´t care, or maybe he was an impressive sociologist who had us all fooled, but not wanted to be seen talking, or laughing.

The game, which I present today, consisted of the following: a dozen people sat around a table and wrote three tests in small roles that were mixed distributed. The tests should be simple, strange and not insulting.

So, you could read in those tests:

- Get closer to the door, from inside the classroom, and start knocking on the door until someone opens it, or until the teacher gets bored of you knocking.
- Sit next to a girl and begin to speak in an invented language.
- Walk in circles around the class, if the teacher is going to sit you down, run away from him slowly, very slowly. The slower you can.
- Look out the window and waves to all passers-by, loudly. You have to be visible.

Play this game with your friends as you get a chance. Having a coffee, some drinks, walking down the center of your town or when having dinner. Any place is perfect for ridicule. The world will not end if you walk around with a Burger King crown for an entire afternoon.

Why is this challenge worth doing? What do I get out of it?

When you face for the first time a hundred people in an audience, when you have to defend an idea against a group of people, or when you have to be the first to interrupt a meeting, you thank having exercised shamelessness and adaptation to any type of test not matter how absurd it was.

How many times have you failed to do something because of what people may think about you? Being shameless, if you are not, it is something that is achieved with practice.

Chapter 35. Not everything that matters is important.

Since we are kids we are taught that we must learn to prioritize in life. We need to know what time to catch the bus or to whether we should reject a task or not at work.

And the truth is that most of us have no idea of how to prioritize. Obviously the experience is important, but let us start from the fact that we have the tool of age in our favor, and we need a mechanism to not screw up systematically in every new project we undertake.

What tool am I bringing you? Your imagination, nothing more What tool am I bringing you? Your imagination, nothing more.

The best way to solve a priority is contemplating both alternatives and their consequences. What will happen if I choose A? What if I choose B? What do I lose if I choose one or another? The challenge today is to analyze the first problem that comes to your head, from shaving your hair to zero, to getting a tattoo done, leaving work, creating a blog, ...

Why is this challenge worth doing? What do I get out of it?

A system to make quick decisions in a graphical way if you want to. The important thing here is to solve a dichotomy, and to think about the consequences of both choices is the best step to reach an acceptable point. Perhaps the answer is mixed and not seen it or it neither convinces us.

Chapter 36. Imaginary Timeline

I want you to do an exercise that, when I did it, got me to smile. Imagine a series of incidents perpetrated by someone, small short phrases like "Subject + verb + complement" something like the ones I am proposing below. I have omitted the subject, do not panic. Imagine that these events happen one after another (although we dont know the time between them).

- He has a fight.
- He falls in love.
- He breaks up with her partner.
- He has a baby.
- He goes to Cancun, he always wanted to go there.
- He has just bought his first car.

I want you to take a moment to think about what kind of person you think our protagonist is. What do those bits of his/her life tell you about him/her? Can you draw a conclusion? Would you be able to deduce how is this person like?

Now do the following. Imagine you meet someone else but you talk about your life in reverse order. That is, read the above quotes from bottom to top. Has something changed in your perception of that person? Is it the same as before? What is different? We receive from the people around us a segmented vision. To get a more complete vision is in our hands.

Why is this challenge worth doing? What do I get out of it?

Have you ever drawn a conclusion about a person from something that he/she has told you about his own life? For example if the person tells you sentence number 2 and number 4 that person is a gentle family man. If number 4 goes after number 5 it gives the impression that something suspicious has happened. If number 1 is before 3 it suggests that the fight has been with his wife.

Now imagine what you know of people you have just met, and you've already tried. Was he justified the trial or want more information.

Chapter 37. Snipe Hunting

Have you ever been in a summer camp? One of those to whom your parents send you to breathe easy for a few weeks a year during summer.

I have, and I believe that in every single one there was someone pranking kids with "Snipe Hunting"

The game is as follows: You give a bag to a newcomer and you fill it up with stones, telling him that they are snipes and he should not open the bag just in case they scape.

The poor boy ends up at 2 am alone with a massive bag full of stones. Funny eh?

Our challenge today will be to not let anyone put those metaphorical stones in our mental pockets. Do not take anything for granted. If you can and have the time to, verify it.

Why is this challenge worth doing? What do I get out of it?

You won´t imagine how many "Snipes" are out there. They can be shown as offers, amazing cars, friends that have done better than you, tricksters.

Is not about looking every night under your bed to see if there are monsters waiting for you….

…. But at least do it for a couple of days everytime you change your mattress.

Chapter 38. Invent a board game

Okay, I know it's not easy to invent a board game. But don´t worry, I'll give you a few tricks that will help a lot with this test. If you don´t come up with any what we will do is to modify existing ones.

Have you ever played any of these games? Chess, checkers, dominoes, ...

Chess, for instance, is one of the classic strategic games with most possibilities. Even if you haven´t ever played certainly you will know the board. Eight boxes per side, two players, thirty-two pieces and many many rules. Too complicated? Try to simplify it.

Imagine the board only consists of four boxes, or simply imagine that it consists of 20 boxes, or it is U shaped.

Why is this challenge worth doing? What do I get out of it?

Surely you've heard of Game Theory or strategies. These little mind games, which some areas of knowledge base them only on mathematics, make us see decisions in another way, and lead us to think beyond the present movements. This will come in handy in life.

Do you think you can create a chess game for three people? If you succeed, I'd love to play.

Chapter 39. You are unique, just like everyone else

Today we play a fairly complex mental game. Believe me when I say that this is one of the few challenges that you may not be able to perform because of its complexity.

Have you ever heard about putting yourself on someone else´s shoes? That is what we will be doing now.

Nobody should be shocked or scared, you won´t need to dissect anyone or do anything weird like Men in Black where an alien changes to a certain Edgard as if it were a suit. It is simply (because the concept is simple) to try to see through the eyes of someone their problems or how they see life in general.

To do so, therefore, we need a person other than you. And yourself, of course.

Now we need something a little more complex: their problems, dreams, desires. What is going through his mind today? Where does he live? Does he take a long subway ride to his house? How does he feel being among many people as I am comfortably alone in my car? Ask yourself as you wish. The more questions you ask the more you will be able to be in someone else´s shoes, to deduct their situation, to change the point of view and extrapolate other ways of thinking.

Why is this challenge worth doing? What do I get out of it?

- that person is in love
- that person is stressed because they won´t have a job
- that person has a bad situation at home
- that person can´t afford his debts
- that person is going to become a father/mother
- that person has just won the lottery.
- …

Have you ever looked at your colleague at work and thought, will he be in love with someone?

This exercise won´t only help you to get a new perspective, but also to learn to know the people through the questions we ask ourselves pretending that we put ourselves in their shoes. Seeing through the eyes of another person not only opens the mind, but requires us to work it. For example: you get comfortably (or not) in your car to the office, but, and what about who travels two hours by train to get there? What time do he have to wake up? What time does he need to go to bed?

Chapter 40. Borrow a book from someone. Now read it

We are used to reading what entertains us or even not to read. Culture has been focused on reading as entertainment, or pleasure.

But there is a wide range in this art, and one of the key things is reading to learn. How many times have you found that overnight (and at home) you have to read umpteen pages for work purposes? A manual, a decree that affects you, your boss´ work or a colleague´s. As of me, from time to time there have been two hundred pages of documents on my desk waiting or in the mail with a "To be finished tomorrow" as subject.

We must open the mind to a type of Reading not based on pleasure, but on learning (although it may be boring and tedious).

So the challenge today is to borrow a random book to someone close. When asked what kind of book say that the first thing they pick at home, no matter what the subject. He will look at you funny, of course. You may (or may not) give this book to him / her as way of explanation. Of course you must read what he gives you.

Why is this challenge worth doing? What do I get out of it?

Bare in mind that the more you worked on reading comprehension, the easier it will be to identify the main ideas in a text, and the faster you will read. The comprehension and understanding are practiced, and not innate. And although it might be easier for some people, no one was born with a language built in his mind.

Putting this into a work related perspective, is it better to read 40 dense pages in an afternoon or having to ask someone for a summary? Everything that you get from doing this yourself will be professionalism and autonomy.

This challenge is focused on the need for reading in the workplace, yet to read and understand every subject is not easy, and will be a powerful tool in your day to day. Practice it. And, easily, you'll do it better.

Marcos Martínez @euklidiadas

Chapter 41. Think laterally

This book focuses on many methods of lateral thinking. However I wanted to write this specific chapter to talk about it.

Lateral thinking is based on problem solving or seeing different situations in a way that, although it is away from the intuitive logical way of thinking, it will resolve equally (or even better) the problem we have.

This is not easy. Looking at a situation from another point of view is terribly complicated. Look at the NASA. When we talk about this organization we think of incredibly smart people (probably all of them wear glasses) known to handle any situation. However, when we talk about the Russians, the first thing that comes to our mind is exactly what appears in online videos: alcoholics who are usually forced by their insurance front camera in their car because of the crazy things they do.

Believe it or not, NASA didn´t invest but spent millions in trying to invent a pen to write in zero gravity. If you've ever written more than two lines on a paper against the wall with the pen in vertical you'll have an idea of the American problem. The Russians solved it using a pencil. Okay, it is not proven and it may be an urban legend, but it is something that may have happened and you would believe me if it had been on the news.

When you have a problem, try to see the bigger picture. The solution to a major problem (or with more perspectives) can be much better. This does not mean that there is a better solution at a lower cost, but there will always be an alternative solution to your problem and that will solve others, although

Do something different

maybe more expensive.

Problem: pens don't work in space, we need to invent one that does. Solution: invest millions.

Broader problem: I need to write in space. Solution: use a pencil.

Why is this challenge worth doing? What do I get out of it?

Looking at alternative solutions will help us in every aspect of our lives. And I do not mean to give the best solution to your boss project or saving the world from a meteorite using a very large catapult. No. I mean you manage better, to select the right temperature of your microwave to spend less (this will always be based on your wife's views, if you have one), or buy the most suitable car.

Problems of everyday life, trying to solve them in a different way, can become a great advantage.

Chapter 42. Hyperchicken theory

When, early last century, we dreamed of space colonization, literally hundreds of theories emerged. From disassemble asteroid belts to transport water in huge tanks.

But there is a theory that, at first glance, it seems silly, not considered and quite absurd, one of those a child could propose in seconds if you ask him something complex.

The theory is this: we launched a "Super Chicken" against Mars to make it habitable. The "Super chicken" does the following: it feeds from the Martian surface, excreting oxygen, water and seeds. And every now and then, he reproduces himself without a partner, with only the sun's energy. In this way hundreds of years would have an habitable Mars.

Obviously a century ago the word 'robot' meant nothing, but scientists had already clear that it should be a mix between an animal and something else the thing that colonizes Mars. Today the most feasible theory to obtain Martian colonization is by fungi or bacteria that will do what our Super Chicken was going to do but at a microscopic scale.

A wild theory or a bright idea? Obviously I'm not going to ask you today to solve the Mars colonization, but…

Now the challenge: locate a problem without current technological solution. O philosophical. O ethical. Now fix it as you can. And if I were you I would record it somehow. It might be necessary in fifty years.

Why is this challenge worth doing? What do I get out of it?

We are square minded. Most of the problems we encounter in life can be solved. And that means that someone before us solved it and created a method. You need to be the next one.

By solving impossible problems you make your brain to move within an unreliable field in which theories are everything and there is no good solution.

Solving these problems helps us see some common problems, and we will create deductive tools that we can use in real life problems.

Examples that you can solve: What can we do about the energy problem? With overpopulation? With pollution? And ... Mars?

Chapter 43. Teach, though at first you do not know how

I have worked as a tutor for years, teaching a variety of technical subjects, and if there is something I have taken is that the best way to learn any subject is teaching it.

This seems incongruous. How do you teach about something you do not know? FYI when I was 16 and I was in high school I started teaching mathematics (algebra and calculus) and technical drawing (graphic expression) to students who had by that time my current age (26 years). And I did it because I needed money and was paid very well.

Since I've lived this experience I always give a tip for all job interviews. When asked if you know about something that you actually have no fucking idea say that there won´t be any problem. Do not say yes, that would be a lie, and you don´t want to lie in a job interview ... you lie to your friends and at home. But insist that you won´t have any problem with it.

As you leave the interview, even if you think you were useless, dedicate 100% of your free time to that you did not know. In less than a week you will have a decent knowledge. In a month you will be someone who knows enough about it, and you will be great on that in a future interview. If you are caught for the position and continuing to learn on your own it will take you less than three years to be a true expert in the field. With much effort, of course. That is, that we assume to teach us something to ourselves.

So the next time you see someone sweating because he can not make his tax report or is unable to program the TV, run to his aid, learn and teach.

Why is this challenge worth doing? What do I get out of it?

Back to the topic at hand, teaching about any subject will provide us expertise, autonomy (we had to fetch information and teach ourselves), confidence in ourselves (there is no subject that can´t be learned).

When we do something for ourselves we grow much better. Have you heard the expression "drawn up the pieces"? It relates to this chapter. Nobody is born knowing, everything you know now you learned it yourself or was taught by someone else.

Chapter 44. Apply theory to practise

The whole idea of this book is to introduce you to a number of tools through a series of exercises to try to see the world from a new perspective.

We always learn theoretical examples applicable to many problems in life, but nobody tells us what problems will be, or what theorem or phrase fits into each. The biggest problem you will encounter appear some random Tuesday at ten o'clock, and no one will help you.

To solve this I bring you today an adaptation (arguably so) of a mathematical theorem that it is possible you may know. It's called Bolzano's Theorem and I have included 3 examples in order of increasing absurdity.

"Mathematics does not apply to real life."

I think this has been the position of many people over many years. Why learn theoretical mathematics if I can not apply them to everyday life? If I simply do addition, subtraction, multiplication and division, and, besides that, I can use the calculator, why bother learning it? I'd rather forget about it and say I am not good at it, I fail every semester and I quit thinking about learning more..

What is that Bolzano 's Theorem? (Strictly speaking, this is the boring bit)

If a real-valued function f is continuous on a closed interval [a, b], differentiable on the open interval (a, b), and f(a) =f(b), then there exists at least one c in the open interval (a, b) such

Do something different

that

$$f'(c) = 0$$

This version of Bolzano's theorem is used to prove the mean value theorem, of which Bolzano's theorem is indeed a special case. It is also the basis for the proof of Taylor's theorem.

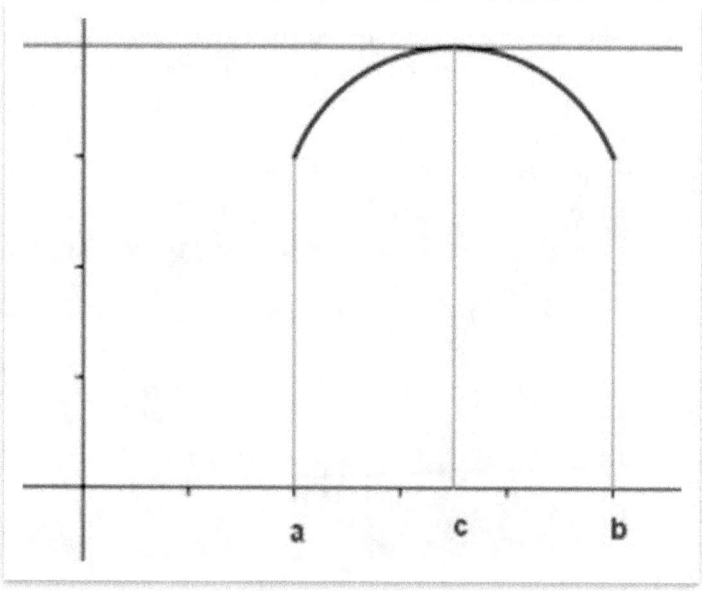

The graphical interpretation of Bolzano's theorem tells us that there is a point where the tangent is parallel to the abscissa.

For those who have not understood: And what the hell does that mean?

The truth is that it's pretty obvious what Bolzano said, but he used mathematical formulas to confuse everyone in a similar to what artists do with their painting when described like "The Emperor's New Clothes". So you see the formulas, letters and encrypted signs and all you can say is:

"It is going to be right this such Bolzano because he seems very smart."

Example 1. The river

Picture yourself on one side of a river long enough to not see its beginning or end (as often happens with almost every self-respecting river). This river has also been kind enough to have always a constant width and no curling itself. For example the following part of Copea river:

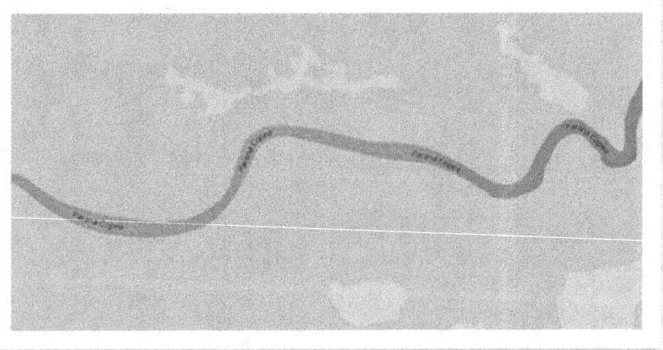

Bolzano's Theorem apologizes because if you want go cross the river (unless you have a flying machine) you will get wet. All that maths theory says you are going to get wet.

Obviously this is something anyone could have told you like:

A builder: "You can´t cross a river without getting wet, you´d rather build a bridge"

Do something different

Fisherman: "You can´t cross a river without getting wet, but the most important thing is what you get from it"

Your mother: "Stay away stupid boy, you will end up getting wet"

Example 2. I don´t want to live anymore, I will jump

Oddly enough many people commit suicide in the world. And a large percentage of them use large buildings or structures, mountains, canyons, or any opening in the ground to jump to a lower level in hopes of getting down and smash (yes, there is such a word) into the ground.

If we see the trajectory of the fall we can ensure various aspects of it. For example, it is continuous and passing through each and every one of the floors of the building before reaching the ground. Bolzano's Theorem shows that, or we learn to fly in a few seconds or we'll smash our head helplessly on the ground, equivalent to the "y = 0".

Example 3. Love

But not all is pure physics or suicidal materialism, Bolzano's theorem can also be applied to such abstract aspects (chemically) as love. Surely you've been in love at some point in your life, and a time before that you were not. Thus it can be argued:

"If you're in love now and a year ago you were not, at some point in the last year you fell in love."

$f(a)$ = not in love

$f(c)$ = falling in love

$f(b)$ = in love

That is, there is a point in time (maybe you have no idea when) that you fell in love.

I imagine that Bolzano didn't have those applications in mind. Honestly, and for the sake of scientific branches of knowledge, I hope so.

Now it´s your turn to find another use for this and other theorems. In my blog you will find other twists to other theorems if you need more inspiration: Bernoulli's principle, double entry accounting, solar radiation, ...

Do something different

Why is this challenge worth doing? What do I get out of it?

In many books you will see great personal learning phrases like "Be whatever you want to be", "only you can decide where you are going to get", etc.

But apart from that, they are nothing. Phrases. Of course they have a practical utility, but would it be too much to ask for an example? Mathematics tells us that for every theorem there is always endless examples. Real life works exactly the same way

I hope you find examples of the dynamics of the book. To help you I have placed this theorem that surely Rolle wasn't expecting to be used like this.

Chapter 45. "Finish that, we will speak later"

How many times have you been interrupted in the middle of a moment of concentration and you felt that after that you have lost the whole morning?

What we will practice today is this: we will not bother anyone if we can. And believe me it is very unlikely you will need to disturb someone to do your job.

If so three different events may be occurring:

- You are new;
- Your job depends on a necessary interaction;
- You are not good at it, you should consider if you are where you should be.

If you are 1 or 2 and you have no choice, interrupt the person when they go for a coffee, or after hanging up the phone. Not in the middle of concentration. This is very important because as Acosta demonstrated with his theorem: "The time required for a task grows when we interrupt and resume it."

Today we will play not to bother anyone.

Why is this challenge worth doing? What do I get out of it?

It will seem incredible, but when you face problems without any help you improve quicker than if you're disturbing your boss every half an hour.

We surround ourselves with people whom you we delegate. On the last trip with my friends I made it clear that I did not want to organize anything, but obviously I would pay. I wasn´t in the mood for organising, and if I had been called to give advise I would have been annoyed as I was in the middle of my mental vacation.

For this I paid and left in the hands of another person everything, trusting his judgment, under the slogan "If I do not think, the plan will look good to me.".

Chapter 46. Do something you would like someone did for you

In contrast to that sentence that your mum repeated everyday, ("Don't do what you wouldn't like to be done "), I expose a reverse concept. What kind of book would this one be if it did not came back to the sayings?

All of us like to be given gifts, being told thousands of nice words, ie, we love to receive things. I suggest you try to give a little bit of you every day and experience what it feels like if every time you do something for yourself and another person at the same time.

It may be something material such as a pair of movie tickets, a book that you knew you wanted to read or a custom shirt; or something more sentimental such as a letter, an unexpected hug (this will always be a good gift, believe me) or a homemade dinner. Whatever it is you choose, however minimal detail, it will sure to pluck a smile to the other person. And that will be the target of the challenge today: collect smiles. The more smiles the better.

I'm pretty sure that once you have been taking something with someone and thought "What would it cost to someone buy me a coffee?", When the focus should probably be: "What will it cost me to invite you to a coffee if we are every two months and every time I do I enjoy great?. "And if that person has never invited you do not mind, stop thinking about what others do for you and think about what you want to do for others. Maybe after that the other person will invite you more often or will thank you in some way. Giving a plug at work, for example. And it's not about selfishness awaiting a bonus by the

Do something different

other person.

Funny how often, for education, will we hold the door for a stranger to pass before us and only rarely do it for a friend, someone who we really matters. You can change that. Let's play to stop thinking selfishly.

Why is this challenge worth doing? What do I get out of it?

We tend to look out through our eyes and see an aggressive world, where there is little external help. We see everything from victimhood: whole planet seems to conspire against you.

How about if we are the agent do not think anyone else that? Bring someone coffee today. Or at all. How many people work with you? Eight people? Eight eight euros and have smiles along one day, or even more.

Chapter 47. Motivate yourself

We are our own fuel. At least at an emotional level.

Usually we tend to look for the push to keep working hard on others, or on the outside in a more generic way, when in reality we have a potential that can make us give 100% all day without these external factors. Listening to people like Emilio Duró or Sergio Fernández gives us the strengh, but the ideal situation would be to have that potential ourselves.

I recently went up the stairs. In the first step there was written "-0,5kcal" in the second "0.7 kcal" and so on. The staircase told you how many calories you had spent depending on the steps you took. Definitely a masterpiece of self-motivation.

Well, with the challenge of today we will search for sentences, slogans, sayings, or simple jokes, comments, pictures, etc, to help you, to motivate yourself, and to tell you, mentally, that you must keep working to get what you want .

It may be a way to remember your goals, for example.

Why is this challenge worth doing? What do I get out of it?

Sometimes, in our work or during our training periods, we forget our ultimate goal. It came a time years where I did not understand why I kept doing all these exercises until I realised "Hey, this is not a combination of exercises, this is a degree".

The next day I wrote with huge letters in my file:

STUDY A LOT, AND SOON WILL YOU BE AN ENGINEER

It was not true, I had to study twice as "much" and it wasn´t quick, but certainly helped a lot more than if I had not written anything.

Chapter 48. Practical uses of super powers.

I am a geek, I can not help it. In fact I do not want to avoid it. A few years there was a TV series called Heroes, where a few humans had unrealized skills such as flying, teleporting, stopping time, and many more imaginative absurdities that filled my head and much of my friends. Obviously all fantastically exaggerated, absurd and incredibly bundled plots and characters that are far from the people I meet on the subway.

What is the challenge behind this unconventional introduction?

When we see a bread oven, almost everyone could think in an imaginative way: "Hey! In there you can make bread. ". And we are not well wrong, but we could give a few more uses that deviate from the buns and pizza (I know, it's hard to get away from them).

We could, for example, use it to heat metal to change its internal structure. Or to melt those plastic soldiers. I see no practical use to this, but the possibility is there.

Well, now imagine one of these characters. The first one we can choose is a guy that is used to move objects with his mind. This is called telekinesis, and again obviously, it is fantasy. When we think of this skill we can all imagine ourselves moving cars, containers, people, etc. But what happens on a smaller scale? We could, for example, strain our phone in the pocket of someone, and that's a helluva trick. O empty a swimming pool to clean it drop by drop. Or we could drive without using your hands, feed in case of quadriplegia or tidy up the room without touching anything with our hands. Telekinesis would be the panacea of chemists or people that work in a car repair service, who come home with smelling and stained hands.

The challenge today is to seek all possible uses of a superhero power.

Why is this challenge worth doing? What do I get out of it?

When we observe the world around us we see a myriad of objects designed for a specific purpose. What if we could give it another use?

This challenge requires great imagination, as rather than objects we will try to raise various uses to concrete and imaginary skills. Therefore it is a pure mental exercise, no practical application in real life but that makes us raise realistic options. From the idea of "The Invisible Man" people have invented invisibility vests, maybe you can become rich.

Unless, of course, that you can move objects with your mind. In that case you can dedicate yourself to clean pools.

Chapter 49. Ask for help

We have focused so far (although if you start the book by this page not) in personal amelioration due to ourselves. In self teaching us to learn.

What if we can teach others or others teach us? How do we do it? The answer is clear: ask for help or opinion.

Asking for help is seen in all areas as a sign of weakness, lack of ability or aptitude. I will say in defense of this that I manage accounting because I asked for help about ten times to different people. Finally, at a certain time someone got accounting explained the way I needed it, as if I were a little boy with a particularly low IQ. With a vocabulary as simple as: "Here in this box, you put where money comes from and where it goes here." I got to understand something in which I had totally lost months and I had read more books than I'm willing to admit.

So when you have a problem, get advice or opinion. Thus you will learn to listen, and the other person to explain. Today we will ask someone for help.

Why is this challenge worth doing? What do I get out of it?

Well, to begin with, if you ask for help, you will get an answer that you did not have before and probably was driving you mad. Remember that not all of us have the same skills. Until recently, writing was a nightmare to me, because I was totally unable to describe any thoughts. Until I met a teacher of Literature (in college, going volunteer, you see...) who was kind enough to sit ten minutes after each class and explain, as if I had a stroke, concepts again and again.

Thanks to this and other people to whom I asked for help I now call myself a writer. And it would have never happened if I had not asked for help. In fact the translation of this book is a purely collaborative work with assistants of various nationalities.

Chapter 50. Be wrong on purpose. Apologize

Apologizing is the unfinished business of virtually everyone. When was the last time you heard "sorry, it was my fault"? Why do we fear being wrong?

Among other things: fear of reprisals, fear of disliking, fear of being judged by that error and people will think you will make it again.

The process of error (because it is documented, and a friend has told me)

1. We make the mistake:

Not necessarily on purpose: forgetfulness, carelessness, a call that you did not make. And suddenly, it is made.

2. We realize

This is the phase of cold sweats. Has anyone else seen it? Has anyone noticed? Can I fix it without being seen? At this time we adopt the attitude of meerkats. With all the discretion that gives a whole body upright on a meadow we start to investigate the questions above.

3. We try to cover it / correct it.

In a display of imagination we act like dogs, "if I bury it, no one will see it." And that is when you can apply the saying "The murderer always returns to the crime scene." It's in our genes, we can not avoid correcting our mistakes if we can, and above all without asking for help (see Chapter 49).

4. If we get caught, we answer with excuses.

A whole range of behaviors from the "I do not know what you're talking about" to "I´m not listening" when someone speaks aloud about the error. The whole office / family / group of friends know who it is: the one that has the spine as a steel bar that prevents from turning the neck around and has eyes looking sideways, like horses.

What seems clear is that mistakes give a bad image, it is not fashionable, and not professional. I'm not asking you to go in search of the error as if seeking the crash to defraud the insurance, but when it happens, be honest. Say it was you. Then, only then, try to correct it or try to avoid it next time.

Why is this challenge worth doing? What do I get out of it?

As I started: apologizing is our unfinished task. We live (actually it is biological) thinking that we are right and the rest not. When we're wrong, we blame others and never ourselves.

Admitting guilt not only will give points against people you know, but helps us seeing the various situations from different perspectives not often seen.

Chapter 51. (this is a gift). Say the same thing but in a different way

How many times we have been told the same way a concept without explaining the main idea?

Being able to explain the same concept intuitively helps not only to be more effective facing an audience, but helps to understand a concept. And, you learn to see it differently.

Explained with an example, so you can visualize it, related to me:

1. Bending concept "complex", or how it should not be taught:

In Engineering bending is the type of deformation that an elongate structural element presents in a direction perpendicular to its longitudinal axis.

2. Concept of bending explained for idiots (which, please, is how I need to be spoken to from now on):

If you push something large in this way (drawing below) it bends like the second picture. If you push it more it will bend more until it breaks, and, depending on which part you are pushing, it will bend more to one side or the other.

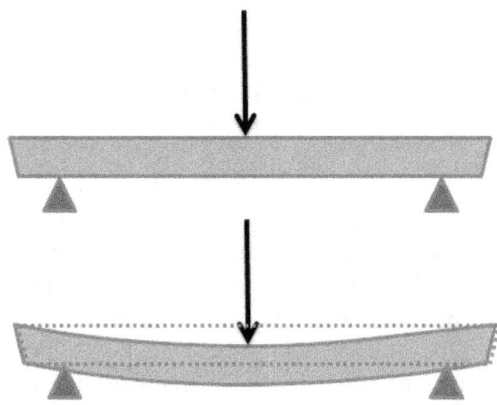

Why is this challenge worth doing? What do I get out of it?

To say we are squared minded is not enough. The brain is designed to be rigid, non-plastic, and, as our example metal bar, it will go back to its original position if you stop pushing.

That is why we must overcome the breakpoint of the brain, pushing ideas until you hear a "click" that tells us that, finally, we managed to learn something. And the best way to learn is to teach (see Chapter 43). So the next time someone asks you to explain anything, be patient and explain things as I do.

Nothing is free, honey

They say nothing is free in life, and unless you are given a 100 euros note by a random person, they are right. There is nothing free in life, and if you are given something for free, the person who has given it to you will expect something later, not necessarily from you.

You may have this book for free from the website. Believe me, I am the first who claims that the cultural sector has changed and requires adaptation. That's why I give this book as cheaply as I can from the website, so you can read it and distribute it. Moreover, I do not know if anyone has noticed the alteration of the beginning text registration of the book, in which I authorize as author to spread their content freely.

For some time I go to a leisure place for free movie tickets. So it seems. All you have to do is sign up for fifteen euros and with that you can go 24 times a year to the cinema. I think it is worth it.

Where's the trick?

As I said before, no one gives anything for free. The objective of this facility is to spread through my name and the brand, buying tickets through people that spread the word and, incidentally, enter to the store every week when we collect our tickets to buy something.

The challenge of this book was, for me, bring some money home, and by you buying it has made this possible. Thank you.

Begin something (that´s all)

It is possible that this is the last challenge you read. Or maybe not. Yes, I know, you have got 3 as gifts. I'm a generous guy. If you have started the book around here, welcome. People do not usually start at the end, but hey, do with this book as you please.

Try opening your eyes all you can and look around. You know what all the objects you see have in common? Buildings, asphalt, traffic lights, the clothing store and clothes they sell, mannequins, countertops, windows and mirrors, each of the vehicles in the street and every one of the objects that hundreds of people carry around you.

All of them have a common point: someone, somewhere, thought it would be good idea to start a project that was to create the object in question. All of them have in common that "someone" that began creating them.

So if you have a project in mind, as it once was this book, begin it. Never mind what others may think or may stop thinking. Use your free time after work to make your project and make it work.

Thank you and congratulations

If you get here, and you have not skipped any exercise, is that you are a person with resistance, initiative and eager to work. What can´t you do from now on? Who knows, maybe write a book, sign up in a sports team or go to ballet lessons. Why not?

I want to thank you again for reading me.

I would love you to leave a comment on my website of which you thought of the book, what have you taught yourself, learnt from others. And I'd like to ask you a favor: share your opinion on social networks, or even better on the website where you bought the book. That would help me incredibly, and takes just a couple of clicks and two lines of text.

It is possible that you are reading this book because you have borrowed it from someone, something that will never disturb me. That´s why it is a digital copy. But note that I make my living with this. It would be great, if you like, to share and come into my blog:

www.pensamientolateral.org

Or my Amazon Page:

Amazon Page

I hope this book has helped you to improve and learn about yourself. It is one of the objectives for which it was written. See you later in the upcoming books.

Do something different

I promise humor, and drama, a bit of inconsistency and much more lateral thinking.